The Philosophy
of Mormonism

By James E. Talmage

ISBN: 978-1-63118-542-7

Mormon History
Series

Other Books in this Series and Related Titles

Pearl of Great Price by Joseph Smith (978-1-63118-539-7)

The Angel of the Prairies or A Dream of the Future: Mormon History Series
By Elder Parley Parker Pratt (978-1-63118-541-0)

The Book of Abraham: Mormon History by George Reynolds (978-1-63118-540-3)

The Testament of Abraham by Abraham (978-1-63118-441-3)

The Book of Parables by Enoch (978-1-63118-429-1)

The Secrets of Enoch by Enoch (978-1-63118-449-9)

American Indian Freemasonry by A C Parker (978-1-63118-460-4)

Lost Chapters of the Book of Daniel and Related Writings (978-1-63118-417-8)

The Book of the Watchers by Enoch (978-1-63118-416-1)

Book of Dreams by Enoch (978-1-63118-437-6)

The Hymns of Hermes by G. R. S. Mead (978-1-63118-405-5)

The Book of Astronomical Secrets by Enoch (978-1-63118-443-7)

The Two Great Pillars of Boaz and Jachin by A Mackey &c (978-1-63118-433-8)

The Regius Poem or Halliwell Manuscript by King Solomon (978-1-63118-447-5)

The Lost Keys of Freemasonry or The Secret of Hiram Abiff (978-1-63118-427-7)

Brothers & Builders by Joseph Fort Newton (978-1-63118-506-9)

Freemasonry, Mithraism and the Ancient Mysteries by various (978-1-63118-407-9)

The Ceremony of Initiation: Analysis & Commentary (978-1-63118-473-4)

The Symbols and Legends of Masonry by C H Vail (978-1-63118-504-5)

The Janeites, The Man Who Would Be King and Other Stories of Freemasonry
by Rudyard Kipling (978-1-63118-480-2)

Audio Versions are also available on Audible, Amazon and Apple

Other Books in this Series and Related Titles

The Hidden Mysteries of Christianity by Annie Besant (978–1–63118–534–2)

Rosicrucian Rules, Secret Signs, Codes and Symbols by various (978-1-63118-488-8)

History and Teachings of the Rosicrucians by W W Westcott &c (978-1-63118-487-1)

Freemasonry and the Egyptian Mysteries by C. W. Leadbeater (978-1-63118-456-7)

The Sepher Yetzirah and the Qabalah by M P Hall (978-1-63118-481-9)

The Psalms of Solomon by King Solomon (978-1-63118-439-0)

The Historic, Mythic and Mystic Christ by Annie Besant (978–1–63118–533–5)

Masonic and Rosicrucian History by M P Hall & H Voorhis (978-1-63118-486-4)

The Kabbalah of Masonry & Related Writings by E Levi &c (978-1-63118-453-6)

Some Deeper Aspects of Masonic Symbolism by A E Waite (978-1-63118-461-1)

Masonic Symbolism of King Solomon's Temple by A Mackey &c (978-1-63118-442-0)

The Old Past Master by Carl H Claudy (978-1-63118-464-2)

The Influence of Pythagoras on Freemasonry and Other Essays (978-1-63118-404-8)

The Mysteries of Freemasonry & the Druids by various (978-1-63118-444-4)

Masonic Symbolism of the Apron & the Altar by various (978-1-63118-428-4)

The Book of Wisdom of Solomon by King Solomon (978-1-63118-502-1)

Masonic Symbolism of Easter and the Christ in Masonry (978-1-63118-434-5)

The Odes of Solomon by King Solomon (978-1-63118-503-8)

Ancient Mysteries and Secret Societies by M P Hall (978-1-63118-410-9)

The Golden Verses of Pythagoras: Five Translations (978-1-63118-479-6)

Freemasonry & Catholicism by Max Heindel (978-1-63118-508-3)

A Few Masonic Sermons by A. C. Ward &c (978-1-63118-435-2)

Audio versions are also available on Audible, Amazon and Apple

Table of Contents

The Philosophy of Mormonism

CHAPTER I

In this attempt to treat the philosophy of "Mormonism" it is assumed that no discussion of Christianity in general nor of the philosophy of Christianity is required. The "Mormon" creed, so far as there is a creed professed by the Latter-day Saints, is pre-eminently Christian in theory, precept, and practise. In what respect, then, may be properly asked, does "Mormonism" differ from the faith and practise of other professedly Christian systems--in short, what is "Mormonism?"

First, let it be remembered that the term "Mormon," with its derivatives, is not the official designation of the Church with which it is usually associated. The name was originally applied in a spirit of derision, as a nick-name in fact, by the opponents of the Church; and was doubtless suggested by the title of a prominent publication given to the world through Joseph Smith in an early period of the Church's history. This, of course, is the Book of Mormon. Nevertheless, the people have accepted the name thus thrust upon them, and answer readily to its call. The proper title of the organization is "The Church of Jesus Christ of Latter-day Saints." The philosophy of "Mormonism" is declared in the name. The people claim this name as having been bestowed by revelation and therefore that, like other names given of God as attested by scriptural instances, it is at once name and title combined.

The Church declines to sail under any flag of man-made design; it repudiates the name of mortals as a part of its title, and thus differs from Lutherans and Wesleyans, Calvinists, Mennonites, and many others, all of whom, worthy though their organizations may be, elevating as may be their precepts, good as may be their practises, declare themselves the followers of men. This is not the church of Moses nor the prophets, of Paul nor of Cephas, of Apollos nor of John; neither of Joseph Smith nor of Brigham Young. It asserts its proud claim as the Church of Jesus Christ.

It refuses to wear a name indicative of distinctive or peculiar doctrines; and in this particular, it differs from churches Catholic and Protestant, Presbyterian, Congregationalist, Unitarian, Methodist and Baptist; its sole distinguishing features are those of the Church of Christ.

In an effort to present in concise form the cardinal doctrines of this organization, I cannot do better than quote the so-called Articles of Faith of the Church of Jesus Christ of Latter-day Saints, which have been in published form before the world for over half a century.[1]

> 1. We believe in God, the Eternal Father, and in His Son, Jesus Christ, and in the Holy Ghost.
>
> 2. We believe that men will be punished for their own sins, and not for Adam's transgression.

---

[1] For extended treatment of "Mormon" doctrine see "The Articles of Faith: a Series of Lectures on the Principal Doctrines of the Church of Jesus Christ of Latter-day Saints," by James E. Talmage. Published by the Church: Salt Lake City, Utah; 485 pp

3. We believe that, through the atonement of Christ, all mankind may be saved, by obedience to the laws and ordinances of the gospel.

4. We believe that the first principles and ordinances of the gospel are: First, Faith in the Lord Jesus Christ; second, Repentance; third, Baptism by immersion for the remission of sins; fourth, Laying on of hands for the gift of the Holy Ghost.

5. We believe that a man must be called of God, by prophecy, and by the laying on of hands, by those who are in authority, to preach the gospel and administer in the ordinances thereof.

6. We believe in the same organization that existed in the primitive church, namely, apostles, prophets, pastors, teachers, evangelists, etc.

7. We believe in the gift of tongues, prophecy, revelation, visions, healing, interpretation of tongues, etc.

8. We believe the Bible to be the word of God, as far as it is translated correctly; we also believe the Book of Mormon to be the word of God.

9. We believe all that God has revealed, all that he does now reveal, and we believe that he will yet reveal many great and important things pertaining to the Kingdom of God.

10. We believe in the literal gathering of Israel and in the restoration of the Ten Tribes; that Zion will be built upon this [the American] continent; that Christ will reign personally upon the earth, and that the earth will be renewed and receive its paradisiacal glory.

11. We claim the privilege of worshiping Almighty God according to the dictates of our own conscience, and allow all men the same privilege, let them worship how, where, or what they may.

12. We believe in being subject to kings, presidents, rulers and magistrates, in obeying, honoring and sustaining the law.

13. We believe in being honest, true, chaste, benevolent, virtuous, and in doing good to all men; indeed we may say that we follow the admonition of Paul, We believe all things, we hope all things, we have endured many things, and hope to be able to endure all things. If there is anything virtuous, lovely, or of good report or praiseworthy, we seek after these things.-- JOSEPH SMITH.

This brief summary of "Mormon" doctrine appears over the signature of Joseph Smith--the man whom the Latter-day Saints accept as the instrument in divine hands of re-establishing the Church of Christ on earth, in this the Dispensation of the Fulness of Times. Let it not be supposed, however, that these Articles of Faith are, or profess to be, a complete code of the doctrines of the Church, for, as declared in one of the "Articles," belief in continuous revelation from Heaven is a characteristic feature of "Mormonism." Yet it is to be noted that no doctrine has been promulgated, which by even strained interpretation could be construed as antagonistic to this early declaration of faith. Nor has any revelation to the Church yet appeared in opposition to earlier revelation of this or of by-gone dispensations.

To most of the declarations in the Articles of Faith, many sects professing Christianity could confidently pledge allegiance; to many of them, all Christian organizations could and professedly do subscribe. Belief in the existence and powers of the Supreme Trinity; in Jesus Christ as the Savior and Redeemer of mankind; in man's individual accountability for his doings; in the acceptance of sacred writ as the Word of God; in the rights of Worship according to the dictates of conscience; in all the moral virtues;--these professions and beliefs are as a common creed in the realm of Christendom. There is no peculiarly "Mormon" interpretation, in the light of which these principles of faith and practise are viewed by the Latter-day Saints, except in a certain simplicity and literalness of acceptance--gross literalness, unrefined materialism, it has been called by some critical opponents.

The gospel plan as accepted and taught by the Latter-day Saints is strikingly simple; disappointing in its simplicity, indeed, to the mind that can find satisfaction in mysteries alone, and to him whose love for metaphor, symbolism, and imagery are stronger than his devotion to truth itself, which may or may not be thus embellished. The Church asserts that the wisdom of human learning, while ranking among the choicest of earthly possessions, is not essential to an understanding of the gospel; and that the preacher of the Word must be otherwise endowed than by the learning of the schoolmen. "Mormonism" is for the wayfaring man, not less than for the scholar, and it possesses a simplicity adapting it to the one as to the other. A few of the characteristically "Mormon" tenets may perhaps be profitably considered.

"Mormonism" affirms its unqualified belief in the Godhead as the Holy Trinity, comprising Father, Son, and Holy Ghost; each of the three a separate and individual personage; the Father and the Son each a personage of spirit and of immortalized body; the Holy Ghost a personage of spirit.

The unity of the Godhead is accepted in the literal fulness of scriptural declaration--that the three are one in purpose, plan and method, alike in all their Godly attributes; one in their divine omniscience and omnipotence; yet as separate and distinct in their personality as are any three inhabitants of earth. "Mormonism" claims that scriptures declaring the oneness of the Trinity admit of this interpretation; that such indeed is the natural interpretation; and that the conception is in accord with reason.

We hold that mankind are literally the spiritual children of God; that even as the Christ had an existence with the Father before coming to earth to take upon himself a tabernacle of flesh, to live and to die as a man in accordance with the fore-ordained plan of redemption, so, too, every child of earth had an existence in the spirit-state before entering upon this mortal probation. We hold the doctrine to be reasonable, scriptural

12

and true, that mortal birth is no more the beginning of the soul's existence than is death its end.

The time-span of mortal life is but one stage in the soul's career, separating the eternity that has preceded from the eternity that is to follow. And this mortal existence is one of the Father's great gifts to his spiritual children, affording them the opportunity of an untrammeled exercise of their free agency, the privilege of meeting temptation and of resisting it if they will, the chance to win exaltation and eternal life.

We claim that all men are equal as to earthly rights and human privileges; but that each has individual capacity and capabilities; that in the primeval world there were spirits noble and great, as there were others of lesser power and inferior purpose. There is no chance in the number or nature of spirits that are born to earth; all who are entitled to the privileges of mortality and have been assigned to this sphere shall come at the time appointed, and shall return to inherit each the glory or the degradation to which he has shown himself adapted. The gospel as understood by the Latter-day Saints affirms the unconditional free-agency of man--his right to accept good or evil, to choose the means of eternal progression or the opposite, to worship as he elects, or to refuse to worship at all--and then to take the consequences of his choice.

"Mormonism" rejects what it regards as a heresy, the false doctrine of pre-destination as an absolute compulsion or even as an irresistible tendency forced upon the individual toward right or wrong--as a pre-appointment to eventual exaltation or condemnation; yet it affirms that the infinite wisdom and fore-

13

knowledge of God makes plain to him the end from the beginning; and that he can read in the natures and dispositions of his children, their destiny.

"Mormonism" claims an actual and literal relationship of parent and child between the Creator and man--not in the figurative sense in which the engine may be called the child of its builder; not the relationship of a thing mechanically made to the maker thereof; but the kinship of father and offspring. In short it is bold enough to declare that man's spirit being the offspring of Deity, and man's body though of earthy components yet being in the very image and likeness of God, man even in his present degraded--aye, fallen condition--still possesses, if only in a latent state, inherited traits, tendencies and powers that tell of his more than royal descent; and that these may be developed so as to make him, even while mortal, in a measure Godlike.

But "Mormonism" is bolder yet. It asserts that in accordance with the inviolable law of organic nature--that like shall beget like, and that multiplication of numbers and perpetuation of species shall be in compliance with the condition "each after his kind," the child may achieve the former status of the parent, and that in his mortal condition man is a God in embryo. However far in the future it may be, what ages may elapse, what eternities may pass before any individual now a mortal being may attain the rank and sanctity of godship, man nevertheless carries in his soul the possibilities of such achievement; even as the crawling caterpillar or the corpse-like chrysalis holds the latent possibility, nay, barring destruction, the certainty indeed, of the winged imago in all the glory of maturity.

"Mormonism" claims that all nature, both on earth and in heaven, operates on a plan of advancement; that the very Eternal Father is a progressive Being; that his perfection, while so complete as to be incomprehensible by man, possesses this essential quality of true perfection--the capacity of eternal increase. That therefore, in the far future, beyond the horizon of eternities perchance, man may attain the status of a God. Yet this does not mean that he shall be then the equal of the Deity he now worships nor that he shall ever overtake those intelligences that are already beyond him in advancement; for to assert such would be to argue that there is no progression beyond a certain stage of attainment, and that advancement is a characteristic of low organization and inferior purpose alone. We believe that there was more than the sounding of brass or the tinkling of wordy cymbals in the fervent admonition of the Christ to his followers--"Be ye therefore perfect, even as your Father which is in heaven is perfect." (Matt. 5:48.)

But it is beyond dispute that in his present state, man is far from the condition of even a relatively perfect being. He is born heir to the weaknesses as well as to the excellencies of generations of ancestors; he inherits potent tendencies for both good and evil; and verily, it seems that in the flesh he has to suffer for the sins of his progenitors. But divine blessings are not to be reckoned in terms of earthly possessions or bodily excellencies alone; the child born under conditions of adversity may after all be richly endowed with opportunity, opportunity which, perhaps, had been less of service amid the surroundings of luxury. We hold that the Father has an individual interest in his children; and that surely in the rendering of divine judgment, the conditions under which each soul has lived in mortality shall be considered.

"Mormonism" accepts the doctrine of the Fall, and the account of the transgression in Eden, as set forth in Genesis; but it affirms that none but Adam is or shall be answerable for Adam's disobedience; that mankind in general are absolutely absolved from responsibility for that "original sin," and that each shall account for his own transgressions alone; that the Fall was foreknown of God--that it was turned to good effect by which the necessary condition of mortality should be inaugurated; and that a Redeemer was provided, before the world was; that general salvation, in the sense of redemption from the effects of the Fall, comes to all without their seeking it; but that individual salvation or rescue from the effects of personal sins is to be acquired by each for himself by faith and good works through the redemption wrought by Jesus Christ. The Church holds that children are born to earth in a sinless state, that they need no individual redemption; that should they die before reaching years of accountability, they return without taint of earthly sin; but as they attain youth or maturity in the flesh, their responsibility increases with their development.

According to the teachings of "Mormonism," Christ's instructions to the people to pray "Thy Kingdom come, thy will be done, on earth as it is in heaven" was not a petition for the impossible, but a fore-shadowing of what shall eventually be. We believe that the day shall yet come when the Kingdom of God on earth shall be one with the Kingdom in heaven; and one King shall rule in both. The Church is regarded as the beginning of this Kingdom on earth; though until the coming of the King, there is no authority in the Church exercising or claiming temporal rule or dominion among the governments of earth. Yet the Church is none the less the beginning of the Kingdom, the germ from which the Kingdom shall develop.

And the Church must be in direct communication with the heavenly Kingdom of which the earthly Kingdom when established shall be a part. Of such a nature was the Church in so far as it existed before the time of Christ's earthly ministry; for the biblical record is replete with instances of direct communication between the prophets and their God. The scriptures are silent as to a single dispensation in which the spiritual leaders of the people depended upon the records of earlier times and by-gone ages for their guidance; but on the contrary, the evidence is complete that in every stage of the Church's history the God of heaven communicated his mind and will unto his earthly representatives. Israel of old were led and governed in all matters spiritual and to a great extent in their temporal affairs by the direct word of revelation. Noah did not depend upon the record of God's dealings with Adam or Enoch, but was directed by the very word and voice of the God whom he represented. Moses was no mere theologian trained for his authority or acts on what God had said to Abraham, to Isaac, or to Jacob; he acted in accordance with instructions given unto him from time to time, as the circumstances of his ministry required. And so on through all the line of prophets, major and minor, down to the priest of the course of Abia unto whom the angel announced the birth of John who was to be the direct fore-runner of the Messiah.

When the Christ came in the flesh he declared that he acted not of himself but according to instructions given him of the Father. Thus the Messiah was a revelator, receiving while in the flesh communication direct and frequent from the heavens. By such revelation he was guided in his earthly ministry; by such he instructed his disciples; unto such he taught his apostles to look for safe guidance when he would have left them.

During his earthly ministry Christ called and ordained men to offices in the Church. We have a record of apostles particularly, numbering twelve, and beside these, seventy others who were commissioned to preach, teach, baptize and perform other ordinances of the Church. After our Lord's departure, we read of the apostles continuing their labors in the light of continued revelation. By this sure guide they selected and set apart those who were to officiate in the Church. By revelation, Peter was directed to carry the gospel to the Gentiles; which expansion of the work was inaugurated by the conversion of the devout Cornelius and his household. By revelation, Saul of Tarsus became Paul the Apostle, a valiant defender of the faith. Holy men of old spake and wrote as they were moved upon by the Holy Ghost and depended not upon the precedents of ancient history nor entirely upon the law then already written. They operated under the conviction that the living Church must be in communication with its living Head; and that the work of God, while it was to be wrought out through the instrumentality of man, was to be directed by him whose work it was, and is.

"Mormonism" claims the same necessity to exist today. It holds that it is no more nearly possible now than it was in the days of the ancient prophets or in the apostolic age for the Church of Christ to exist without direct and continuous revelation from God. This necessitates the existence and authorized ministrations of prophets, apostles, high priests, seventies, elders, bishops, priests, teachers and deacons, now as anciently--not men selected by men without authority, clothed by human ceremonial alone, nor men with the empty names of office, but men who bear the title because they possess the authority, having been called of God.

Is it unreasonable, is it unphilosophical, thus to look for additional light and knowledge? Shall religion be the one department of human thought and effort in which progression is impossible? What would we say of the chemist, the astronomer, the physicist, or the geologist, who would proclaim that no further discovery or revelation of scientific truth is possible, or who would declare that the only occupation open to students of science is to con the books of by-gone times and to apply the principles long ago made known, since none others shall ever be discovered?

The chief motive impelling to research and investigation is the conviction that to knowledge and wisdom there is no end. "Mormonism" affirms that all wisdom is of God, that the halo of his glory is intelligence, and that man has not yet learned all there is to learn of him and his ways. We hold that the doctrine of continuous revelation from God is not less philosophical and scientific than scriptural.

CHAPTER II

The Latter-day Saints affirm that the authority to act in the name of God--the Holy Priesthood--has been restored to earth in this dispensation and age, in accordance with the inspired predictions of earlier times. But, it may be asked, what necessity was there for a restoration if the Priesthood had been once established upon earth? None indeed, had it never been taken away. A general apostasy from the primitive Church is conceded in effect by some authorities in ecclesiastical history; though few admit the entire discontinuance of priestly power, or the full suspension of authority to operate in the ordinances of the Church. This great apostasy was foretold. Paul warned the Saints of Thessalonica against those who claimed that the second coming of Christ was then near at hand: "For," said he, "that day shall not come except there come a falling away first." (II Thess. 2:3.) "Mormonism" contends that there has been a general falling away from the Church of Christ, dating from the time immediately following the apostolic period. We believe that the proper interpretation of history will confirm this view; and, moreover, that the inspired scriptures foretold just such a condition.[2]

If the Priesthood had been once taken from the earth no human power could re-establish it; the restoration of this authority from heaven would be necessary. The Church claims

---

[2] See "The Great Apostasy: Considered in the Light of Scriptural and Secular History," by James E. Talmage. Published by the Deseret News, Salt Lake City, Utah; 176 pp.

that in the present age this restoration has been effected by the personal ministrations of those who exercised the authority in earlier dispensations. Thus, in 1829, Joseph Smith and Oliver Cowdery received the Lesser or Aaronic Priesthood under the hands of John the Baptist, who visited them as a resurrected being--the same Baptist who by special and divine commission held the authority of that Priesthood in the dispensation of the "Meridian of Time." Later, the Higher or Melchizedek Priesthood was conferred upon them through the personal ministrations of Peter, James, and John--the same three who constituted the presidency of the apostolic body in the primitive Church, after the departure of the Lord Jesus Christ by whom it was founded.

That the claim is a bold one is conceded without argument. The Church of Jesus Christ of Latter-day Saints professes to have the Priesthood of old restored in its fulness; and, moreover, while acknowledging the right of every individual as of every sect or other organization of individuals to believe and practise according to choice in matters religious, it affirms that it is the only Church on the face of the earth possessing this authority and Priesthood; and that therefore it is The Church and the only Church of Christ upon the earth today. It holds as absolutely indispensable to proper Church organization, the presence of the living oracles of God who shall be directed from the heavens in their earthly ministry; and these, "Mormonism" asserts, are to be found with the Church of Jesus Christ.

"Mormonism" emphasizes the doctrine that that which is Caesar's be given unto Caesar, while that which is God's be rendered unto him. Therefore, it teaches that all things pertaining unto earth, and unto man's earthly affairs, may with propriety be regulated by earthly authority, but that in the performance of any ordinance, rite, or ceremony, claimed to be of effect beyond, the grave, a power greater than that of man is requisite or the performance is void. Therefore, membership in the Church, which, if of any value and significance at all, is of more than temporal meaning, must be governed by laws which are prescribed by the powers of heaven. "Mormonism" recognizes Jesus Christ as the head of the Church, as the literal Savior and Redeemer of mankind, as the King of kings and Lord of lords, as the One whose right it is to reign on earth, who shall yet subdue all worldly kingdoms under his feet, who shall present the earth in its final state of redemption to the Father. It is his right to prescribe the conditions under which mankind may be made partakers of his bounty and of the privileges of the victory won by him over death and the grave.

The Church claims that faith in God is essential to intelligent service of him; and that faith, trust, confidence in God as the Father of mankind, as the Supreme Being to whom all shall render account of their deeds and misdeeds, must lead to a desire to serve him and thus produce repentance. Faith in God and genuine repentance of sin, of necessity, therefore constitute the fundamental principles of the gospel. It is reasonable to expect that after man has developed faith in God, and has repented of his sins, he will be eager to find a means of demonstrating his sincerity; and this means is found in the requirement concerning baptism as essential to entrance into the Church, and as a means whereby remission of sins may be

23

obtained. As to the mode of baptism, the Church affirms that immersion alone is the one method sanctioned by scripture, and that this mode has been expressly prescribed by revelation in the present dispensation.

Water baptism, then, becomes a basic principle and the first essential ordinance of the gospel. It is to be administered by one having authority; and that authority rests in the Priesthood given of God. Following baptism by water, comes the ordinance of the bestowal of the Holy Ghost by the authorized imposition of hands, which constitutes the true baptism of the Spirit. These requirements, designated specifically the "first principles and ordinances of the gospel," "Mormonism" claims to be absolutely essential to membership in the Church of Christ, and this without modification or qualification as to the time at which the individual lived in mortality.

Then with propriety it may be asked:--What shall become of those who lived and died while the Priesthood was not operative upon the earth?--those who have worked out their mortal probation during the ages of the great apostasy? Furthermore, what shall be the destiny of those who, though living in a time of spiritual light, perhaps had not the opportunity of learning and obeying the gospel requirements? Here again the inherent justice of "Mormon" philosophy shows itself in the doctrine of salvation for the dead. No distinction is made between the living and the dead in the solemn declaration of the Savior to Nicodemus, which appears to have been given the widest possible application,--that except a man be born of water and of the spirit he cannot enter into the Kingdom of God. (John 3:1-5.)

"Mormonism" proclaims something more than a heaven and a hell, to one or the other of which all spirits of men shall be assigned, perhaps on the basis of a very narrow margin of merit or demerit. As it affirms the existence of an infinite range of graded intelligences, so it claims the widest and fullest gradation of conditions of future existence. It holds that the honest, though, perchance, mistaken soul who lived or tried to live according to the light he had received, shall be counted among the honorable of the earth, and shall find opportunity, if not here then in the hereafter, for compliance with the requirements essential for salvation. It teaches that repentance with all its attendant blessings shall be possible beyond the grave; but that inasmuch as the change we call death does not transform the character of the soul, repentance there will be difficult for him who has ruthlessly and willfully rejected the manifold opportunities afforded him for repentance here. It asserts that even the heathen devotee who may have bowed down to stocks and stones, if in so doing he was obeying the highest law of worship which to his benighted soul had come, shall have part in the first resurrection, and shall be afforded the opportunity, which on earth he had not found, of doing that which is required of God's children for salvation. And for all the dead who have been without the privileges, perhaps indeed without the knowledge, of compliance with Christ's law, there shall be given opportunity in the hereafter.

Nevertheless, this life of ours is no trifle, no insignificant incident in the soul's eternal course, having but small and temporal importance, the omissions of which can be rectified with ease by the individual beyond the veil. If compliance with the divine law as exemplified by the requirements of faith, repentance, baptism, and the bestowal of the right to the ministrations of the Holy Ghost, are essential to the salvation of those few who just now are counted among the living, such is not less necessary for those who once were living but now are dead. Who are the living of today but those who shortly shall be added to the uncounted dead? Who are the dead but those who at some time have lived in mortality?

Christ has been ordained to be judge of both quick and dead; he is Lord of living and dead as man uses these terms, for all live unto him. How then shall the dead receive the blessings and ordinances denied to them or by them neglected while in the flesh? "Mormonism" answers: By the vicarious work of the living in their behalf! It was this great and privileged labor to which the prophet Malachi referred in his solemn declaration, that before the great and dreadful day of the Lord, Elijah should be sent with the commission to turn the hearts of the fathers to the children and the hearts of the children to the fathers. Elijah's visitation to earth has been realized. On the 3rd of April, in the year 1836, there appeared unto Joseph Smith and Oliver Cowdery, in the temple erected by the. Latter-day Saints at Kirtland, Ohio, Elijah the prophet, who announced that the time spoken of by Malachi had fully come; then and there he bestowed the authority, for this dispensation, to inaugurate and carry on this labor in behalf of the departed.

As to the fidelity with which the Latter-day Saints have sought to discharge the duties thus divinely required at their hands, let the temples erected in poverty as in relative prosperity--by the blood and tears of the people--testify. Two

26

of these great edifices were constructed by the Latter-day Saints in the days of their tribulation, in times of their direst persecution,--one at Kirtland, Ohio, the other at Nauvoo, Illinois. The first is still standing, though no longer possessed by the people who built it; and no longer employed for the furtherance of the purposes of its erection; the second fell a prey to flames enkindled by mobocratic hate. Four others have been constructed in the vales of Utah, and are today in service, dedicated to the blessing of the living, and particularly to the vicarious labor of the living in behalf of the dead. In them the ordinances of baptism, and the laying on of hands for the bestowal of the Holy Ghost, are performed upon the living representatives of the dead.[3]

But this labor for the dead is two-fold; it comprises the proper performance of the required ordinances on earth, and the preaching of the gospel to the departed. Shall we suppose that all of God's good gifts to his children are restricted to the narrow limits of mortal existence? We are told of the inauguration of this great missionary labor in the spirit world, as effected by the Christ himself. After his resurrection, and immediately following the period during which his body had lain in the tomb guarded by the soldiery, he declared to the sorrowing Magdalene that he had not at that time ascended to his Father; and, in the light of his dying promise to the penitent

---

[3] For a detailed treatment of Temples and Temple labor among the Latter-day Saints, including a study of the doctrine of vicarious labor for the dead, see "The House of the Lord, a Study of Holy Sanctuaries Ancient and Modern," including forty-six plates illustrative of modern Temples; by James E. Talmage. Published by the Church: Salt Lake City, Utah; 336 pp.

malefactor who suffered on a cross by his side, we learn that he had been in paradise. Peter also tells us of his labors--that he was preaching to the spirits in prison, to those who had been disobedient in the days of Noah when the long-suffering of God waited while the ark was preparing. If it was deemed necessary or just that the gospel be carried to spirits that were disobedient or neglectful in the days of Noah, are we justified in concluding that others who have rejected or neglected the word of God shall be left in a state of perpetual condemnation?

"Mormonism" claims that not only shall the gospel be carried to the living, and be preached to every creature, but that the great missionary labor, the burden of which has been placed on the Church, must of necessity be extended to the realm of the dead. It declares unequivocally that without compliance with the requirements established by Jesus Christ, no soul can be saved from the fate of the condemned; but that opportunity shall be given to every one in the season of his fitness to receive it, be he heathen or civilized, living or dead.

The whole duty of man is to live and work according to the highest laws of right made known to him, to walk according to the best light that has been shed about his path; and while Justice shall deny to every soul that has not rendered obedience to the law, entrance into the kingdom of the blessed, Mercy shall claim opportunity for all who, have shown themselves willing to receive the truth and obey its behests.

It will be seen, then, that "Mormonism" offers no modified or conditional claims as to the necessity of compliance with the laws and ordinances of the gospel by every responsible inhabitant of earth unto whom salvation shall come. It distinguishes not between enlightened and heathen nations, nor between men of high and low intelligence; nor even between the living and the dead. No human being who has attained years of accountability in the flesh, may hope for salvation in the kingdom of God until he has rendered obedience to the requirements of Christ, the Redeemer of the world.

But while thus decisive, "Mormonism" is not exclusive. It does not claim that all who have failed to accept and obey the gospel of eternal life shall be eternally and forever damned. While boldly asserting that the Church of Jesus Christ of Latter-day Saints is the sole repository of the Holy Priesthood as now restored to earth, it teaches and demands the fullest toleration for all individuals, and organizations of individuals, professing righteousness; and holds that each shall be rewarded for the measure of good he has wrought, to be adjudged in accordance with the spiritual knowledge he has gained. For such high claims combined with such professions of tolerance, the Church has been accused of inconsistency. Let it not be forgotten, however, that toleration is not acceptance. I may believe with the utmost fulness of my soul's powers that I am right and my neighbor is wrong concerning any proposition or principle; but such conviction gives me no semblance of right for interfering with his exercise of freedom. The only bounds to the liberty of an individual are such as mark the liberty of another, or the rights of the community. God himself treats as sacred, and therefore as inviolable, the freedom of the human soul.

"Know this, that every soul is free To choose his life and what he'll be; For this eternal truth is given, That God will force no man to heaven.

"He'll call, persuade, direct aright, Bless him with wisdom, love, and light; In nameless ways be good and kind, But never force the human mind."

"Mormonism" contends that no man or nation possesses the right to forcibly deprive even the heathen of his right to worship his deity. Though idolatry has been marked from the earliest ages with the seal of divine disfavor, it may represent in the unenlightened soul the sincerest reverence of which the person is capable. He should be taught better, but not compelled to render worship which to him is false because in violation of his conscience.

In further defense of the Latter-day Saints against the charge of inconsistency for this their tolerance toward others whom they verily believe to be wrong, let me again urge the cardinal principle that every man is accountable for his acts, and shall be judged in the light of the law as made known to him.

There is no claim of universal forgiveness; no unwarranted glorification of Mercy to the degrading or neglect of Justice; no thought that a single sin of omission or of commission shall fail to leave its wound or scar. In the great future there shall be found a place for every soul, whatever his grade of spiritual intelligence may be. "In my Father's house are many mansions," (John 14:2), declared the Savior to his apostles; and Paul adds, "There are also celestial bodies, and bodies terrestrial; but the glory of the celestial is one, and the glory of the terrestrial is another. There is one glory of the sun and another glory of the moon and another glory of the stars; for one star differeth from another star in glory. So also is the resurrection of the dead," (I Cor. 15:40-42). The Latter-day Saints claim a revelation of the present dispensation as supplementing the scripture just quoted. From this later scripture (see D&C, Sec. 76), we learn that there are three well-defined degrees in the future state, with numerous, perhaps numberless, gradations.

There is the celestial state provided for those who have lived the whole law, who have accepted the testimony of the Christ, who have complied with the required ordinances of the gospel, who have been valiant in the cause of virtue and truth. Then there is the terrestrial state, comparable to the first as is the moon to the sun. This shall be given to the less valiant, to many who are nevertheless among the worthy men of the earth, but who perchance have been deceived as to the gospel and its requirements. The telestial state is for those who have failed to live according to the light given them; those who have had to suffer the results of their sins; those who have been of Moses, of Paul, of Apollos, and of any one of a multitude of others, but not of the Christ.

We hold that there is a wide difference between salvation and exaltation; that there are infinite gradations beyond the grave as there are here, and as there were in the state preceding this.

"Mormonism" is frequently spoken of as a new religion, and the Church as a new church, a mere addition of one to the many sects that have so long striven for recognition and ascendency among men. It is new only as the springtime following the darkness and the cold of the year's night is new. The Church is a new one only as the ripening fruit is a new development in the course of the tree's growth. In a general and true sense, "Mormonism" is not new to the world. It is founded on the gospel of Christ which antedates this earth. The establishment of the Church in the present age was but a restoration. True, the Church is progressive as it ever has been; it is therefore productive of more and greater things as the years link themselves into the centuries; but the living seed contains within its husk all the possibilities of the mature plant.

This so-called new, modern gospel is in fact the old one, the first one, come again. It demands the organization and the authority characteristic of the Church in former days, when there was a Church of God upon the earth; it expects no more consideration, and scarcely hopes for greater popularity, than were accorded the primitive Church. Opposition, persecution, and martyrdom have been its portion, but these tribulations it accepts, knowing well that to bear such has been the lot of the true Church in every age.

"Mormonism" is more than a code of morals; it claims a higher rank than that of an organization of men planned and instituted by the wisdom and philosophy of men, however worthy. It draws a distinction between morality and religion; and affirms that human duty is not comprised in a mere avoidance of sin. It regards the strictest morality as an indispensable feature of every religious system claiming in any degree divine recognition; and yet it looks upon morality as but the alphabet from which the words and sentences of a truly religious life may be framed. However euphonious the words, however eloquent the periods, to make the writing of highest worth there must be present the divine thought; and this, man of himself cannot conceive.

It affirms that there was a yesterday as there is a today, and shall be a tomorrow, in the dealings of God with men; that

Through the ages one increasing purpose runs; and that purpose,--the working out of a divine plan, the ultimate object of which is the salvation and exaltation of the human family.

The central feature of that plan was the earthly ministry and redeeming sacrifice of the Christ in the meridian of time; the consummation shall be ushered in by the return of that same Christ to earth as the Rewarder of righteousness, the Avenger of iniquity, and as the world's Judge.

The Church holds that in the light of revelation, ancient and modern, and by a fair interpretation of the signs of the times, the second coming of the Redeemer is near at hand. The present is the final dispensation of the earth in its present state; these are the last days of which the prophets in all ages have sung.

But of what use are theories and philosophies of religion without practical application? Of what avail is belief as a mere mental assent or denial? Let it develop into virile faith; vitalize it; animate it; then it becomes a moving power. The Latter-day Saints point with some confidence to what they have attempted and begun, and to the little they have already done in the line of their convictions, as proof of their sincerity.

For the second coming of the Redeemer, preparation is demanded of men; and today, instead of the single priest crying in the wilderness of Judaea, there are thousands going forth among the nations with a message as definite and as important as that of the Baptist; and their proclamation is a reiteration of the voice in the desert--"Repent Repent! for the Kingdom of Heaven is at hand."

The philosophy of "Mormonism" rests on the literal acceptance of a living, personal God, and on the unreserved compliance with his law as from time to time revealed.

www.ingramcontent.com/pod-product-compliance
Lightning Source LLC
LaVergne TN
LVHW091322080426
835510LV00007B/610